The Speeding Tortoise

Simons Acquah

Illustrated by H.Likhon

Copyright 2018 by Simons Acquah and Love Legacy Books LLC.

All rights reserved. No part of this book may be reproduced, stored in a retrievable system, or transmitted in any form or by any means- electronic, mechanical, photocopying, recording, or otherwise- without the prior written permission of Simons Acquah and Love Legacy Books LLC.

Simons Acquah
Love Legacy Books
P.O. Box 293
North Beach, MD 20714
U.S.A

To Everyone who is working hard everyday to make a difference in children's lives. The world needs you to keep up the good work.

You are heroes indeed!.

"Too many people overvalue what they are not and undervalue what they are"

-Malcom S. Forbes.

One afternoon, deep in the rain-forest, the sun appeared and everything looked bright. All the animals came out for sunlight. Soon after they gathered, they started telling stories.

Peacock felt left out. "I don't have any stories to share, but surely, I am the most beautiful of all the birds," she said. "I am proud of my feathers, and I attract attention wherever I go."

Eagle said, "I am the most majestic bird, and I can also fly the highest in the sky."

Then Tiger said, "What about me? I have the most beautiful fur, and I am the fastest runner in the forest."

All the creatures took turns bragging about their strengths, accomplishments, and unique qualities.

In their midst was Tortoise. He thought long and hard but couldn't find one thing to brag about. He was very sad, so he quietly left the gathering and sat under a tree. He curled into his shell and cried.

Rabbit saw Tortoise and asked why he was crying. "There is something special about each of the other animals," Tortoise answered, "but there is nothing special about me. I am ugly and slow, with nothing to be proud of."

"That's not true," said Rabbit. "You aren't ugly, and I'm sure there's something special about you. Why don't you go ask Owl? She is wise and will know the answer. She also has magical powers, so even if she doesn't know, she can make you into whatever you want to be."

"That's a great idea," said Tortoise. "I will go find Owl."

"I will come with you," said Rabbit.

The two friends set out together, but on the way, there was a rain storm. Rabbit's fur got wet, which made her cold, and she had to go back to her rabbit hole to get warm.

But Tortoise was determined to reach his destination. His shell kept him warm and dry, so he could stay on the path to Owl's tree.

"What brings you here in the middle of a storm?" asked Owl when Tortoise finally arrived. "It must be really important."

Tortoise told his story again. He explained how all the creatures had something to be proud of, but he had nothing.

Owl was moved. "Why do you think you have nothing? Of course you have something. I can think of many things that are special about you."

"I don't need you to flatter me. I need you to tell me the truth," Tortoise replied. "Is there really something about me that is special and unique?

Owl didn't hesitate. "You are the most careful animal in this forest," she said, "and you have a beautiful shell."

But Tortoise didn't think his shell was beautiful. And being careful didn't seem like something he could brag about.

"Telling me I'm careful is just a nice way of saying I'm the slowest of all creatures," said Tortoise. He felt like crying again.

"Tortoise; many creatures would love to be as careful as you are," said Owl. "It is an advantage."

"No, it's a disadvantage," said Tortoise. "I don't like being slow. I want to be fast. In fact, I want to be the fastest creature ever. Please do some magic for me. I traveled a whole day to see you."

"Well, since you don't see carefulness as a good thing, do you want to exchange that for speed?" asked Owl.

"Yes, I do!" cried Tortoise.

Owl took a magic potion and poured it onto Tortoise, who immediately fell into a deep sleep.

When he opened his eyes the next morning, he saw that he was still under Owl's tree, but Owl was gone.

Every time Tortoise started to move, the speed was too fast for him. He ran into trees, and he ran into rocks. He was so fast that he had no control. He was scared, but also happy that his wish had been granted.

"I just have to learn how to manage this speed, and then I'll be perfect," he told himself.

Soon everyone was talking about Tortoise and his uncontrollable speed. They all wondered what had happened to him. Some envied his new ability, but Tortoise quickly became unhappy.

He was running into trees and rocks everywhere, and his head was always sore. He couldn't stop to talk to any of his friends because by the time he managed to slow down, he was already far past them.

He missed his friend Rabbit a lot, so he decided to not move for days, knowing that if he just

stayed still, she would come find him.

Just as he expected, Rabbit arrived. "Hey! I've wanted to talk to you, but you run by too fast for conversation," she said. "Are you happy now that Owl made you so fast?" But before Tortoise could answer, Rabbit screamed, "What in the world happened to you? Why have you broken your shell into pieces?"

"What do you mean, Rabbit?" Tortoise asked.

"Oh, my friend, I'm sure you haven't seen it yet, but your beautiful shell is broken all over. I am so sorry," said Rabbit.

Tortoise couldn't believe it. Sure enough, his shell was all broken and ruined from moving too fast and bumping into everything.

After Rabbit left, Tortoise decided to return to Owl and ask to be himself again. When he set out, it took him only a few minutes to get there.

"Why have you come back? Are you here to thank me?" asked Owl.

"I came to ask you to help me go back to the way I was," Tortoise replied, sheepishly.

"Oh, no, I can't do that," Owl exclaimed. "I can't reverse such an important wish of yours. And besides, your shell is all cracked and broken. What would be the purpose of being careful now?"

But Tortoise was desperate to be himself again. "Please, Owl, fix my shell and make me slow and careful once more. I'll do whatever you ask."

Owl thought for a moment, then said, "I'll return you to your old self, but only if you promise to be happy with who you are."

"I promise. Oh, I will be!" cried Tortoise.

Owl poured another potion onto Tortoise to put him to sleep.

When he awoke the next morning, his shell was whole again. "It is a beautiful shell," he said to himself, noticing its lovely pattern for the first time. Then he began his slow journey back home, taking care with every step.

The wind began to blow, and suddenly a big tree fell onto the ground right in front of him. "How fortunate that I am slow and careful," he thought. "Had I been a little faster, that tree would have landed on me!"

It took Tortoise a whole day to walk back to his destination, but he was so happy to be himself again. He found Rabbit, and the two of them stayed up all night talking and laughing about everything that had happened.

The end.

Simons Acquah has extensive travel and life experiences which have shaped him to encourage people to live a full life, appreciating opportunities and using passion to make a difference. He is passionate about teaching character building through children's literature.

He has always been fascinated by stories that emphasize lessons we learn from animals like ants, elephants, tortoise and many more. It is truly astonishing the values of hard work, love, unity, honesty and many life lessons he is able to share with children through animals.

Simons was born in Ghana and Lives in North Beach Maryland with his wife Kate and three lovely kids. He has an MBA from Lincoln University, Missouri.

Made in the USA
Monee, IL
14 September 2019